BELIEFS

AND

BLASPHEMIES

BELIEFS
AND
BLASPHEMIES

A Collection of Poems

VIRGINIA HAMILTON ADAIR

RANDOM HOUSE

NEW YORK

Library of Congress Cataloging-in-Publication Data
Adair, Virginia, 1913–
Beliefs and blasphemies : a collection of poems / Virginia
Hamilton Adair.
p.   cm.
ISBN 0-812-99245-8
I. Title.
PS3551.D244B4   1998
811'.54—dc21   97-47403

Random House website address: www.randomhouse.com
Manufactured in the United States of America

To Kappa Waugh and Connie Kimos
a thousand thanks

Contents

PART I

IMAGING A MAKER

Whodunit

Is there some cosmic lab
where the stars conspire, inventing Life?
Did the parturition of nothingness
give birth to all this glory?

The writers of mysteries busy themselves with death.
But who or what is the perpetrator of Life?
We live and die in the eternal question mark.

Goddesses First

From the beginning, they must have been miles ahead of the
        men,
fleet as fawns, nimbly evading those heavy hulks lumbering
        after
giving apelike yells to establish mastery,
their bellies stuffed with animal fat, their lungs caked with
        chewing tobacco.

The escaping female swung up into trees, while her pursuer
broke the branch and toppled into the briars. It is easy to see
why goddesses preceded gods. The female wit was sharper.
God is a girl, they intoned, and if you don't believe us, no soup
        tonight.

The males howled when blood ran from a cut;
the women could bleed mysteriously and feel no pain.
From the place of blood came new beings, small creations of
        great interest.
The men were always fooling around this secret entrance, exit.

Come on in, the girls would say, when warm and well fed.
They found the male huffing and puffing greatly amusing,
like later on, the TV comedian after the dishes and the evening
  news.

In All

Part of the maker dwells in all that's made:
in crafted things, the plough, the ax, the spade,
the everlasting flower carved in jade,
souls of the trees that gather in the glade,
beauty of girls, although their beauty fade,
the starry marchers in the sky parade,
the egg in chaste perfection, newly laid.
The maker dwells in all the maker made.

To the Worldmaker

Why does mankind insist you have a gender?
Are you a scary ruler, punitive yet tender,
jealous and bellicose, with a short fuse,
and partial to an ancient tribe of Jews?

Like Carroll's Cheshire cat, your features fade,
leaving a smile for all the worlds you've made.

Games with God

I played, a child both wild and meek,
with God at games of hide-and-seek.
I searched in vain the usual places
and found a thousand saddened faces.

"Your God is hidden in heaven," they said;
"You'll see him only when you're dead."
How could I make them understand
God often took me by the hand?
Then as my tears began to fall
I felt his touch and heard his call,
"I never hid from you at all."

I played with God a game of tag,
his mantle flying like a flag.
I gave my God a good head start
but caught him running in my heart.

I played with God the game "I Spy,"
but lost him with my fading eye,
till playmate God in his pure kindness,
printed his image on my blindness.

Versions of Jehovah

Versions from Aramaic to Old Greek
only approximate the truth we seek.

Quoth poor Jehovah, frowning as he read,
"They've falsified most everything I said."

Downsize

I
Something has got to happen soon.
The universe continues to expand
and who will stop it?
Not I, said God, with my angel band,
my flowing beard and my upraised hand.
Whose breath inflates this vast balloon?
And who will pop it?

II
Poor Mr. God is out of work;
what agency will feed him?
A single father must not shirk
his duty to five billion kids
who really badly need him.
But poor old God is on the skids
and Mammon must succeed him.

These shocking thoughts we should not tell,
in case there really is a hell.

Easter 1990

Nuns prayed that doves descend,
that pimps and pushers discover Christ,
that nations caught in the steel traps
of dictators find sweet release.
The homeless, experts in failed systems,
prayed under their cardboard blankets.
The munitions-maker's daughter prayed,
poolside or speeding in her Porsche
with the sun as her passenger,
that all the depressing news get lost.

One day God got around to answering
the big backlog of requests.
Uncountable TV's imaged crowds
swaying and screaming in the great squares
of the world. Wounds turned to roses,
open mouths gulped down liberation,
breathing out sighs, "At last, at last!"
Not bombs but salvos of simple happiness
swept over the astounded cities.

It was so sudden, improbable as UFO's:
those months of walls collapsing,
prisons unlocked, prisoners elected rulers,
kites made from constitutions,
treaties torn into confetti.

How soon would the populace falter
without its old hates and horrors?
Without devils would the nations be undone,
skinheads mourn in their useless arsenals?

Not to worry, God has told us
before, knowing our needs well
and how fast our tolerance for joy fails.
His scripts are imponderable,
His serial without end.
A new cast waits in the studio.

Bridge

Shuffle my cardboard selves
with the gay, worn, and dirty backs.
My emblems caper through your fingers.
Do not drop me; but cut me, deal me,
let the combinations form
whether my Here or Heaven be at stake.

Arrange me, masterhand; fan out my forces;
take pleasure in my patterns.
Play me well; I'd lose no trick for you.
Sweep me together surely at the end,
all suits complete, one deck,
winner take all! Take all!

Choosing

You toys of God that wheel and turn,
by His great fingers formed and spun,
the moons that freeze, the suns that burn,
among a million things to praise
I choose your game of nights and days,
all my frail vision can discern:
the darks that loom, the brights that burn,
and see my daughter's outline still
wave like a flower on a hill,
signaling to my fading eye
pure love against the empty sky.

One Only

The winter-fearing heart implores
fire from a touch, a look, a voice;
yet soon the bodies, names, and faces
turn away into empty places.

Only one constancy survives
the passion in the park at dusk,
sustains our transient, troubled lives
beyond the sorrow and the risk.

The unfailing friend for whom we yearn,
emblem of wonder and of light,
more steadily than stars that burn
across infinitudes of night

can flood our winter world with sun,
fill solitude with ecstasy:
lost love, lost hope transformed by One
of love and hope the epitome.

PART II

MANY MANSIONS

Long Beginnings

In my childhood God was unequivocally male:
He, Him, and His capitalized,
and variously described in superlatives.
He was Lord of Hosts, angels with spears presumably,
usurping vengeance, judgments,
punishments as His prerogative.
He was also Jesus, meek and mild.
All very confusing to a thoughtful child.

The Jews seemed to be the authors and promoters
of monotheism, a great cast of characters,
nuggets of wisdom, entrancing tales,
fine roiling sentences in Shakespearean language.
My mother's church, Episcopalian, packaged the whole
    confusion
in splendid ritual, pageantry, and verbiage.
Hellfire smoldered in the background but was not obtrusive,
the smell of sulfur modified by incense, candle wax, and
    Sunday soap.

At camp I found that worship under the trees was good.
I discovered Bach chorales and Negro spirituals.
After many side trips, in my fifty-fifth year I came home
to group meditation, candle and incense reinforced
by wooden clapper, silvery gong, and drum.
Freedom to begin the long search for my creator.

Zen in the Quaker Sunday School

I ZAZEN

When I first floundered in
no one knew me

not even myself
staggering under a Saratoga trunk
crammed with humiliations
bottled like urine samples
nailkegs of anger
carbons of abusive letters
chemistry quizzes with F's
even the horse I never had
and two casseroles left over
from the dime-a-dip supper.

No one remarked that
I had brought too much.

I was wearing 3 fur hats
donated by opulent cousins
my feet encased in cement
ever since the failure
of the patio project
and my mouth full of barbs
as an old trout.

No one praised my appearance.

The trunk fell off my back
disgorging its unusual contents
at my stone feet
which also came off.
The fur hats tumbled like a
motheaten avalanche
burying a small monk.

No one noticed.

My sweat began to dry
I folded myself into one piece

NO ONE . . .

II SANZEN

In a midden
Of plastic cars and dollcrap
The Roshi sits like the Sierras.

He questions, "Koan?"

I emit the miasmas of my culture.

The Roshi clears the air with his fan.
He extends branches.
His eyebrows perch there.

He shakes his bell.

Backing out
I fall into the toybox.

Saving the Songs

Said Luther of the singing in saloons,
"Why should the devil have the choicest tunes?"
He therefore, unless history is a liar,
Moved the best tunes from taproom into choir.

Though some are shocked, the controversy dims
When all the world sings lusty Lutheran hymns.
God's in His heaven, Christmas cheer in barrels,
And 'round the world, the lovely Lutheran carols.

Chichester Cathedral

In the cathedral at Chichester, God came incognito,
putting on gender like an old bathrobe.
The creator of all things visible and invisible
knew the world's need for a kindly grandfather.

So, yielding to popular pressure,
he let the worshipers have their way.
He put on faded carpet slippers,
padded down the stone aisles, smiling vaguely
at the organ's solemn belly rumblings of reverence.

I felt the dead listening from their stone boxes:
longtime residents in their earthly remnants
of bone and shriveled leather,
empty eyesockets staring at eternity.
A stained-glass window told some old tale
repeating itself in colorful light on the worn paving stones.

I bent a knee, sank down onto the uncushioned pew.
It was like having tea with God, companionable,
but with no need to say anything.

On the St. Lawrence

Midnight in a cabin
below the waterline
waiting for the tide.

Montreal, you are still
to me an unknown city.

Only the vast dome of St. Joseph's
Oratory opened its heart
while Bach echoed himself
on the heaven-resounding organ;
and from the vertiginous gallery
you, far city, your parks and river,
seemed cupped in the hand of God.

A billion summer prayers
written on leaves and flowers
quivered between your terrible snows.

The Chapel at Mountain State Mental Hospital

The chapel boasted no stained glass,
no holy relics, shroud of Turin,
no marble tomb or funeral brass,
no incense for the reek of urine.

Attendants, prisoners on parole,
a pair of alcoholic sin-mates,
brought Alice in her camisole
and other oddly costumed inmates,
creaking and thundering on the stair,
the crash of a collapsing chair
competing with the opening prayer.

All types appeared, from crone to bimbo,
pimply youth to hoary gaffer,
chatty fools and ghouls in limbo,
weeper, curser, groaner, laugher,
stylish Steve with arms akimbo.

A dove flew in and out the window
trying to catch a moth and gulp it,
building a nest above the pulpit.
Diane in purple trimmed with ermine
called the male patients "swine" and "vermin"
during the hymn and then the sermon.

A radio was turned up high,
two patients listening to a game;
the bird departed for the sky
when down the aisle an old man came
asking who took up the collection,
and laid an orange upon the lectern.
The sermon went on all the same.

Like *le jongleur de Nôtre Dame,*
Jean made her offering with aplomb;
passing the front row to the aisle,
she turned on God a dazzling smile,
with perfect cartwheels all the while
in a full skirt with streaming hair,
but not one stitch of underwear,
no top except a scarlet halter,
she somersaulted past the altar.
The preacher stopped his peroration
to marvel at each pure gyration;
so did the motley congregation,
and no one tried to make her stop,
till ending, with a bow and hop,
she moved, with hair and clothing neat,
demure and quiet to her seat.

Surely *le jongleur* would relate
to Jean, the cartwheel queen of Mountain State.

Gaffer and girl convert us with their motions
to greater freedom in our own devotions;
the broken windows of the mind may give
the wingèd spirit still a space to live.

Wings Like an Angel

Not far from his own boyhood, the airman flew
over the church, the roofs, and roads he knew.
He saw the range of mountains, white with snow,
and children on a tiny lawn below,
so close, they saw the gloved salute he gave;
he felt them cheering, saw them watch and wave.

Two decades later, and new children race
for life across the target marketplace.
Pity and anger mingled, bittersweet,
he drops his firebombs on the ancient street.
Creatures like burning torches leap and run;
the great rose window shatters in the sun.
And as the shadows of the bombers pass,
Christ dies upon a hill of broken glass.

PART III

YESHUA

From the First

From the first he was there:
before the silence of cells and the hot mist,
at home with his father whom he never saw,
yet knew so surely—
carpenter of creation, engineer of the cosmos—
whom he called "loving."

How could God know he was "love"
before this voice, these eyes, told him?

In the warm night of the womb,
in silence he became a cell.
Much was obscured by being born;
but he did his best to remember to relate
heaven to earth, to impart in the narrow confines
of his place and time some measure of his father's plan.

Some stood there and heard nothing.
They were like students everywhere
thinking of what they would do when the class ended.

But others felt at the touch of his words
death fall from their shoulders like a loosened shroud.
In the dark discomfort of their bones
a sun was born
and they carried this fire in their hands and on their tongues
to the feeble and furious.
Blackness surrendered; the blind saw.

Still the nonlisteners straggled off, uneasy.
Let's set the priests wise to this crowd.
Let's see who's being stoned today.
Let's shoot craps with the soldiers.
You know, I'd like to nail something on that guy.
He makes me nervous.
Nail him to the cross.
As usual the crowd came; the happening made history.

As he did in the beginning
so still he stands at the temporal graveside
or beside the sea in the sunrise
frying a fish, still meets our eyes
above the headlines in the commuter's car.
We are slow to learn, God knows.
But sometimes, yes, our hearts still burn within us.

Yeshua

What's in a name? Oh, plenty, I declare.
Versions of "Jesus" turn up everywhere.
Such variations I suspect appalled you;
Is "Yeshua" the name your parents called you?

For Yeshua

The press photographers were not yet there
to have the makeup artist curl his hair,
and yet that image turns up everywhere.
His followers might have said, "You wouldn't dare
to call our Master 'meek and mild,' 'most fair,'
or dress him in a gown that ladies wear."
Isn't the truth about him *anywhere*?

Making Truth

What stories of your birth night came to you?
Any of those details our childhood knew?
We loved Luke's version, and the legend grew.
Such long believing makes a story true.

If and What

If the Wise Ones came that midnight
(and what an outstanding story)
the innkeeper must have been wild.
"That pair could have paid in gold
but we put them out in the cold,
in the animal fold, for God's sake.
So what if the newborn kid
would keep everybody awake?
Of all impossible things,
who could have guessed that child
might be related to kings?"

If the odd star really marked it
(and what a marvelous fable)
no wonder herdsmen bound for market
stopped at the crowded stable.
No wonder a choir dropped in—
angels, or just the local
off-duty cantor or barbershop four
standing there in the steamy door

to sing for his sake—or a piece of the cake—
but those camels and kings were focal.

If they really brought those chests
of treasure (a lovely tale)
did the parents invest the presents
or cash them in at a sale?
That trip to Egypt for all three
was hard on the ass and not for free.
Surely the child had a right
after outgrowing the kneeling oxes
to know what became of the birthday boxes
he got that night in the barn.
(Just one more thread for the yarn.)

If the three kings paid their call
(and the scene is really great)
no wonder the boy at twelve had a sense of fate—
and likely, too, a sense of doom.
For resin and myrrh are not at all
right for a body fresh from the womb
but more for one dressed for its funeral.
No wonder the Master was wary, there on the Olive hill.
Had you kept that costly incense, Mary?
Did you hoard it still?

The Lost Gospel

(FOR J. R.)

At dawn you give your upper garment
to the wretch shivering by the roadside.
At noon you are knocking on doors;
some open, some slam.
The day smiles on you;
you give thanks for its warmth.
Fever departs from the bedridden one
flowing into the sun
descending its bright ladder into darkness.
You have no food;
but look, a little windfall apple
has rolled into the ditch, offering itself.
You give thanks and eat.

The cold hands of night reach for you
across the desert
and together you whisper to the stars.
All the immensity of darkness draws close
around you, covering you like the garment
you gave away in the dawn.

You are like a child whose father
bends down to comfort him into sleep.

Tomorrow you will walk to a hill
with others following, eager to hear something new.
And the words of blessedness will be blown
on the breath of that simple day,
around and around the world forever and ever.

Sermon on the Sermon

Let us skip for a moment the beatitudes
and get down to the refreshments. The picnic part.
Their souls were already fed; their stomachs were empty.

What had transpired needed talking over
with a mouthful of bread and a swig from the wineskin.
Snacks appeared from nowhere—the fruit, the cookies,
the hardboiled eggs and the peanut-butter sandwiches.

All were shared, traded, divided and relished
like the school lunches in their little tin boxes.
Somehow everyone went away satisfied.

But they would soon discover a new hunger.
To feed the lambs, there was always grass enough.
Feeding the world might be the same:
sharing, trading, buoyed by the words that went before.

Remember the day, the words, the miracle.

Communion

Who spoke the words
now repeated by the priest,
words at the breaking of bread,
ascribed to the Lord of the feast?
Good friends and wine and food,
yet still his heart was sore.

And she who had swept the floor
and, after the making of bread,
had set the board,
did she listen behind the door
to the words many say he said?

Did sorrow pierce her to the bone
for all that lay ahead
causing those tears to flood?
The words are a woman's own
who for her child has borne and bled.

"Mine is the body and the blood
given for you,
first emerging with such strife
down my corridor of life,
mystic daughter, sacred son;
love makes each a holy one."

His Mother

So much is speculation,
goddess-building, evolution
of art from art from art.

He seemed to reject her at one point.
What mother? What brothers?
But she was with him at the end.
Where was Joseph?
(Where was God the Father
for that matter?

Showing up too late for the crucifixion,
tearing the temple veil in a snit,
darkening sky, shaking ground
Jupiter-stuff. Thor-thunder.)

His mother probably had to go home
and clean house.
Feed John, who was always
dropping in
after the Event.
Somehow outlive the horror.

Her most difficult kid,
she always said,
but what a darling!
Something about him too good
for this lousy world.
Don't forget him. Don't forget my boy—
his beautiful voice
saying those strange things.
He could be right, you know,
in the long run.

Veronica

A child finds a soiled scarf
in a chest of heirlooms.

Her mother tells her:
Your great-grandmother Veronica
had a ringside seat
for one of those messy executions.
Jesus wasn't respectable then
as he's getting to be now.
Granny was just a girl
but she reached out and blotted
his bloody face with her new veil.
Her family was furious.
Veronica kept that piece of cloth
all her life. Asked for it at her death.

It had mildewed or something,
like the print of a face.
Granny whispered, "My Lord's face,
I see it," and died smiling.

Put it back, child.
You won't believe this, but collectors
have offered me money
for that old rag.
Inflation being what it is
I'm holding out for a better price.
See the mouth, the eyes?
Granny was quite a girl.

PART IV

ARREST

Pro Snake

Some say the Bible teaches fear of women, snakes,
and God, who killed his manchild for our sakes
and puts a mark beside our least mistakes,
and beats us all until our spirit breaks.

Must we believe his godly finger shakes
at Eve for every apple pie she bakes?
I'd rather take my chances with the snakes.

Seven Deadly Sins

Behold the systematic GLUTTON
who eats the fat first off his mutton,
and while the blessing says, "We're grateful,"
he's asking for a second plateful.

This man is also AVARICIOUS,
finding the smell of dough delicious,
and takes a fierce, uxorious PRIDE
in one possession: his young bride.

His neighbor just across the fence,
a man of strong CONCUPISCENCE,
ENVYING the husband his fair flower,
would buy her favors by the hour.

ANGER inflames the husband's face,
but AVARICE takes the higher place.
He says, "Don't let my ANGER trouble you;
Take her—I'll take your BMW."

The deal is struck; with one car more,
a final sin completes his score.
The sinner says, "I'd shoot them both,
were I not such a slave to SLOTH."

Judas

The devil said, "When I was tempting Jesus,
I told him I could make him rich as Croesus.
But he misjudged my power, the pious scoffer.
His televangelists took up my offer."

Dirty Old Man

A few beers make his mood pugnacious,
his jokes and stories more salacious,
his eye for nymphets more rapacious,
with older women most ungracious;
his appetite for fat, voracious,
swells his manly gut capacious.
With piety somewhat audacious
he calls upon his saint, Ignatius,
"Save me a bed in Heaven so spacious
that it will hold a hundred geishas."

Arrest

Driving down boulevards
toward our private purposes
we see this public monitor
the cop car FLASHING STOP * - * - *
to penalize some luckless
part of a needed quota.

The angel with his holster
sent by THE EYE ABOVE
which redly glowers * - * - *
tears from a ticketbook
the childhood terror CAUGHT.

We slacken speed and sicken
in dull dread of misdeeds: STOPS
we glided through, the fender
nicked unseen (so we thought)
and LIMITS wildly exceeded
in the late, late night.

We quicken, menace pedestrians,
pass passing trucks, unsignaling
turn with an agony of tire
praying he will not behold, pursue,
FLASH STOP * - * - * this messenger

whose car is BLACK AND WHITE
as Sunday fables our forebears
read with tight shoes and hearts.

The Hooker at the Church Picnic

She saw that she had been seen touching the young sailor's fly.
The two cops would drive down the long street, turn at the
    corner,
and come back. The paper bag she carried was still warm.
It was the week of hot cross buns.

She followed a group carrying casseroles up stone steps into
    the churchyard.
She was half sick, half hungry.
She placed her hot cross buns on a platter with somebody's
    Danish.
She accepted a paper plate of baked beans and sat down on
    the grass,
her back against a young tree.

The man in the priest's collar came over to her,
smiled a welcome and asked, "Are you OK?"
Without thinking, she took his hand and held it to her cheek.
"I've been stoned for six days," she said.

The two policemen were at the gate.
He went over to them, laughed, and shook his head; they left.
The woman said, "Jesus."
It always made her sick, people eating wieners.
The priest was about to speak; the crowd fell silent.
"Jesus," she said again, "I guess I was more hungry than sick."

A great peace came over her; she fell asleep
leaning against the tree, and someone's little white dog
licked her plate clean.

Yom Kippur

I
When the Atlantic heaved itself at the sky,
crashed inland, raping the tidal rivers,
my friend told me, "This is the time of atonement."

I have never been sure of meanings
of sin, atonement, forgiveness.
I wonder whether the great spirit knows, itself,
or cares. Whenever I swam in the York River
with its taste of the sea, all my sins,
such as they were, floated away,
and I was ready for new ones.

When the hurricane washed a huge whelk ashore from the
Mattaponi,
I carried it home and kept it three days in a bowl.
But the sacrilege was heavy upon me,
and I drove back thirty miles to return it to its beach,
casting it back to the river god;
it may have been itself the river god.

I think perhaps this was sin and almost instant atonement.
Did you forgive me then, Lord of creation,
River God, Whelk with the strange pulsing foot?
My Yom Kippur guest for three days in a bowl of salted water
waiting for my change of heart.

II
But another transgression has weighed upon me so sadly
that for fifty years I have, yes, atoned in spirit.

It was hot summer when we fished for food,
caught bluegreen crabs, hitching along out of the net,
on their way to the cooking pot. We were hungry and
heartless.

But the day we netted the old turtle and we hung it up
and cut off its head, I was jubilant, then uneasy,
and now uselessly horrified and contrite.
It was so venerable, so huge, lord of its little creek,
watcher of the tides, living, living.

Over and over I have thought: forgive.

Hymn

The four windows of the one-room shack
framed four mountains: Sheephole, Joshua Tree,
San Gorgonio (still snow-crested in April),
and eastward, a hill of white sand that turned pink at sunset.

The man and the girl lay half nude on the bed,
staring out the open door. In the silence,
the wind hummed in the greasewood bushes
and the man was humming softly a hymn tune
she remembered from childhood:
" 'Where every prospect pleases,' " she said,
"I used to think prospect was some kind of candy."

A motorbike engine buzzed not far off and then stopped.
They were both half asleep
when an unexpected footfall made him start up.
A stranger, heavyset, unsmiling, stood in the doorway.
The man, barefoot, went quickly to the door.
"Are you looking for the Browns?
It's two cabins down the crossroad."

The stranger said nothing but stared hard at the girl.
"I won't ask you in," said the man.
"My wife is not feeling well."
"She looks to me like she feels pretty good," said the stranger.
Her husband reached in the camp icebox at the door
and took out a Coke, opened it, and handed it to the other man.
In the desert you don't argue with thirst.
The stranger took it, shook it, holding his thumb over the hole.
He was still looking at the woman.
He released his thumb and the foam spewed out onto the
     doorsill.
"The wetter the better," he said.

The two of them watched in silence as he turned and walked
down the sand road toward his bike.
"Thank you for keeping your temper," she said.
"I had to. He had a gun in his pocket."
"I just thought of the next line," she said.
They laughed then, and sang softly together
the old missionary hymn:
" 'Where every prospect pleases, and only man is vile.' "

Trails to Untruth

The trail to the truth has many a turning
to the place in the plaza with stakes for the burning.

The bishop's tall miters, the guard's lofty shakos
turn flocks from the truth to Guianas and Wacos,
but crush with the crozier and pierce with the sword
the souls who seek answers direct from the Lord.

The scribes in their cells built of bibles and hymnals
surrender the truth to sectarian symbols,
and the vastness of God they delight to compress
into bylaws that only a bigot could bless.

No Mercy

Merciful God, what action did you take
with prelates burning martyrs at the stake
saying they did so for your son's dear sake?

PART V

MINERAL, VEGETABLE, ANIMAL

Matter and Soul

The mountain looks to the sun
talks in shadows to a cloud:
Why do you come between us?

The rock looks to the mountain:
Mother, I broke away.
Do you miss me?

Sands look to the rock
a single grain whispers:
Was I not part of you?

We are so many
you are one.
Dance with us, O God.

Due Reverence

Even the vegetables
      I strongly suspect of having souls.
Someone has suggested
      that the highest joy of the beet
      lies in being eaten, with proper reverence.
Broccoli goes down
      the dark digestive tunnel
      an ecstatic martyr to human need.
And I sense
      the silent scream of the avocado:
      "Save, oh save my splendid seed."

Look, No Feet

A friend rebuked the error of my lines:
How God felt snake one of his best designs.
God hacked off the serpent's little feet
for telling Eve that apples were a treat.
What zealot started this godawful rumor?
I hear God laugh. I love his sense of humor.

A Shell Singing

Water wove me, dawn
    dyed me, sand fed me, a child
        held me to the sun.

A seagull absorbed me,
    soaring from saltfoam into
        the deep swells of cloud.

In my carapace
    I contain oceans, bubbles,
        continents of sand.

Empty of its flesh
    my frame harbors the sea's voice,
        the moon's memory.

Crash through the windows
    of my broken self, bright wave.
        I shake with laughter.

A Kind of Zazen

The mudflat breathes
through a film of blessèd water

Clouds look down
to watch their own wandering

From its hole in the sand
a clam calls to the sea

and the sea comes.

Competing Kingdoms

We furless, trunkless, finless folk invade
the little kingdoms where the beasts still reign.

In some corners of our fading world
their glory still moves and multiplies:
the great white bear
like a moving mountain of snow,
and over the green veldt, a pair of cheetahs
unloosing their incredible swiftness
in pursuit of life and death,
converting one into the other.

Who will save us from ourselves,
our sad solutions of zoos,
electric fences, torture labs?
The whale goes mad in its little tank.
The panther paces eternally back and forth
cursing its cage, calling on its forest god.
The polar bear dreams
of colors marching across her northern heaven.

Grace

Inventor of life,

when the whales surface,
they do homage to the suns
in water and sky.

The eagle soars, slides down air
from heaven, giving thanks
for wings and atmosphere.

The elephants as they feed
trumpet a fanfare signifying
grace before vegetation.

The Birds Preach to St. Francis

[VARIATION ON A THEME BY LISZT]

What could he tell them they did not already know?
Their wings were beating the air
like tongues at Pentecost,
their beaks unrolling ribbons of fire.

"Man," they chorused, "dip and dance as we do
in the eddies of air.
With syllables of jubilation,
stitch earth to paradise."

PART VI

MOMENT

The Recognition

Once across restless mounds of the sea
our eyes met; only the distance and unaccustomed
darkness kept me from Your face
until decades had gone by;

until now, until here,
past so much needless sorrowing
in the bleak places, waiting for forgetful
faces, and forgetting the one look between us

like the flash of pharos to ship's light
over waters drenched with night and danger,
I rediscover,
after so many roads inland and shoreward led nowhere,

the one look that takes all, gives all,

makes hearth henceforth that warmth engendered
by its secret fire in marrow, myriad cells:
those joyous runners in the blood crying, Awake!
the long waiting to begin is over.

Entrance

We have all known, now and then,
that the place is always there, waiting,
ours for the asking,
for the silent stepping out of ourselves
into solace and renewal.

We do not even need a gate,
though it can be pleasantly awesome,
a ritual of entrance.

Some walk straight in,
through the invisible wall of wonder.
Some scramble through a hedge of thorns,
thankful for the pain, the bright drops of blood.
Some enter over the token length of wall;
they like the solid scrape of stone,
the breathless act of climbing.
Once we are in, no matter how,
the secret terrain goes on forever.

When we forget it is there,
then it is gone,
and we are left outside
until we remember.

Moment

On a raft tethered to the Kentucky riverbank,
a child oblivious to my companions,
I lie looking up at a density of leaves
where the golden light of the water shimmers
above me, below me, and I feel the flowing past
of Bluegrass kin from other shores and cultures
in the eternal moment.

And on a granite rock rising
from the cool waters of Georgian Bay
turning aside from first love and the young lovers
suddenly I contain and cherish all humankind
and the hawk overhead, the fish hidden below,
and the beautiful snake sunning
on a nearby rock, my heart hovering
in the eternal moment.

Between walls of golden broom I come
to the beach at Yorktown
neglecting the three miracles from my womb
to lie alone on the sand, blinded
by an immensity of love, by the peace
and passion of the sun, adoring
land, water, sky, all life and mystery
in the eternal moment.

Now in the aridity of my age
on the dry boards of an old porch I lie alone
suspended in the enormous joy of being
still unknowing: is this divine worship
or earthly Eros? The deep chorale
in the pines like far-off surf, like the sigh
of tidal rivers, the tender suck of waves
on moist banks, hum of our spinning planet—
all breathe for me and I for them
in the eternal moment.

Good Night, Good Day

Time the unfathomable is neither foe nor father.

I traveled three thousand miles to walk by the sea
and you put a tiny shell in my hand;
it extended a little foot, stirring on the continent of my palm.

This poem has no ending, and the beginning
goes back a million years.

Enormous Day

Enormous day, wrapt in a maze of light,
upriser from the edge of earth, sea-wanderer,
deep strider down the hills' convexities,
gentle ambassador from Heaven's courts,
be now the signal for our prayers and deeds;
remind us with your noon how love in us
may flood all, may be high and shadowless.

Alone, one, from all eons, moving into night,

unfearing and unwearying, from God's hand
released for flight, and to that hand returning,
lend us your sunset courage at the end;
bright voyager, departing leave us wiser
for your great gift of hours; may we devote
to darkening earth this legacy of light
flashed from the mirrors of our mortal hearts.

The Voice

Suddenly my youth was gone, and my heart was wild.
But the voice at the edge of the night said,
"You no longer need to run and climb like an aging child.
Forget the beach, the woodland and the hill.
There is space for speed and motion still."

Suddenly my sight was gone;
but the voice in the cloudy dawn eased my pain,
telling me, "You will see again in a new way
the lengthening shadow on the lawn, the unseen birds
that bring you in their beaks the newborn day."

Suddenly I was alone, my bed was cold.
The voice in the void said, "Faces you cannot see,
like flowers in a garden will unfold.
Do not call back the joys that cannot stay,
warm hands return more than you gave away."

Suddenly I could no longer hear
my children's voices, once so loud and clear.
And the voice in the echo said,
"Even the words of love will disappear, but do not fear.
Silence will bring reverberations near."

Suddenly then I had no place to live,
but, "You still have much to give.
You will enter an unexpected door,
and I will make you see and be as never before,"
said the voice on the edge of light.

PART VII

BEYOND

The Welcomer

Toby is trotting on ahead,
the click of his paw nails audible
only to the living in their dreams.

Overhead a playtime of cherubic puppies
gather into June clouds and Christmas snowballs.
They hail him: "We are the welcomers.
Soon you too will be a welcomer."

Toby trots on between the high gates
into the everlasting mystery.
He is not awed by the entry,
for he is planning his welcome
to the dear beings whose hands
are baskets of tenderness.

He will do his little four-footed dance of delight,
his *tour jeté* of joy.
He will speak to them in their own language.

All parts of Toby are there,
but free of pain and perplexities.
All the loveliest smells of life
are in the air; and the gray grass
is an unimaginable green.

Already his throat and tongue are forcing
his first human syllable: love.
"And I shall teach them to bark," thinks Toby,
"Alpha and omega! *Hanya haramita!* Tao! Tao! Tao!"

The Playground of the Dead

Do we take a hearse back to childhood
on the playground of the dead,
a dreamland of bats and balls,
wickets and mallets?

(I have heard that memory and soul
are immortal,
truer than blood or bone.)

The new kids come in droves,
shedding their cares and corpses,
their hates and hang-ups.

Ring-around-the-rosy and "London Bridge"
have their old importance again.
Pin the wing on the angel,
who turns out to be the boy next door
we were always at war with.

No crazy killer goes through the open gate
with grenade and gun.
"Come to the playground of the dead," we sing,
swinging from the bars of the jungle gym.
And sooner or later, everyone comes.

So Long

What will we do without words?
In the long game underground
the worms will be the winners.
In the long passage of their bodies
we shall at last learn meekness,
inheritors of the earth, in the end.

Beyond

In the stillness of the cave he stood
unwinding the cloth from his torn body.

Earlier the hired guards had moved the stone a little
to peer in, assure themselves of his death.

He slipped through the narrow aperture
as if in a dream or a prayer.

The opening in his side had closed;
holes in hands and feet were sealed in blood.

He looked back at the men
sleeping beside their empty wineskin.

He was somewhere else now, as if without walking.

The night wind seemed to lift him;
or was it only his hair stirring back from his forehead?

The sea breathed its freshness into his parched lips and lungs.

He stepped into the water, his blood pale roses
floating around his knees.

He began to climb the steps of the sea.

He walked for a while on the surface of the water
among angels of mist.

He rose through a cloud cover into the blue midnight.

This was the blue of a dress his mother used to wear;
her arms seemed to reach out to him as in his childhood.

Now he was walking on a highway of stars.

When he came to a dark portal,
would there not be light beyond?

He stood at the doorway, crying out,
"Father, I have come home."

A Solitary Walk

Toward the end, my father dreamed
often of his brother Tom.
They had been close in age and spirit,
but in this dream, my father walked alone.

The lights in the town behind him
were going out one by one,
each a breath down the chimney
of an oil lamp on the table
of a shuttered house.
He walked barefoot in the cool dust
of the country road that led to his first school—
but who goes to school after dark?

The school had vanished
as the children used to hope it might
before autumn came again.
Now he had come to one
of those farmland gates, with long arms
and a rope pull at the end of each.

You pulled and the arm rose up
and the big gate swung open.

As he stood there in the summer twilight,
the gate faintly white, his heart halted
for the distance of a few breaths,
a few steps, while a mockingbird
in the grove ahead broke into a melodic line
of joy, grief, and unspeakable
tenderness for a lost land.

No need for heartbeat now.
The nightwind, soft as a deep sigh of earth,
carried him through the open gate
and set him down on the far side.
He reached up to the second rope
pulling the gate shut behind him.
He was still alone, but a familiar form
drifted toward him through the grove.
"Tom," he called, "is that you?"

The Gatherer

Through the fields you walk,
cutting the delicate stalk
with your shears, shining-bladed,
the blooms fresh or faded,
carrying against your breast
color, form, and scent.
And who can fathom your intent,
leaving the living rest
to grow, bend, wave, and smile
for a little while, a little while,
as you silently bear away
the flowers you gather for that single day?
And who will miss them from that crowded field?
Only the roots, the plants, that had to yield.

Timing

How can we say "I'm sorry" to the dead?
Say it to God and hope he'll pass it on?
Perhaps it's best to get the "Sorry" said
before the injured ones are dead and gone.

The Reassemblage

Some myths are too terrible for our believing:

that the compendium of all our years and yearning,
that poor bundle of knobby bones and leather,
must wait through millennia as scattered dust,
its bits and pieces digested by worms and beetles?
until the great dictator gives it leave to reassemble
and stand naked to be tried, not by a jury of its peers,
but a judge with far too many cases on His, Her, or Its
agenda?

So the grave was after all a cell on death row.

Now come the rewards and punishments:
one a verdict brutal beyond imagination,
the other by most reports an eternity of boredom.

But billions have lived and died by this myth,
evolved by sadists and masochists,
even by the great John Donne, napping in his coffin,
arrayed in frilled nightcap
just to get the feel of things to come.

Oh, you arbiters of the afterlife, let the soul go on dancing,
the mind exploring, discovering,
setting forth into unending wonders of the universe,
the wilderness of words,
the vast mysteries of the human mind.

Walking into Siberia

You told me, Mary Tarail,
of a night when you lived on the Arctic Circle.
(But wasn't it night most of the time?)
How you set out for supper with a friend
in a nearby cabin,
and suddenly entered a demonic blizzard
sweeping you off course,
canceling compass and even courage.

You said when you tried to go straight,
you were walking into Siberia.
We have all been there, over and over,
one way or another.
You told me a hand reached out in that blind swirling
and led you to the door of light,
the smell of warm food,
voices of friends.

We all retrace one another's wanderings.
Without the unseen eyes, hands, secret directions,
we may sink in the soft snow
to lie lost and powerless.
They say a stealing warmth may flow over us,
and in the last earthly dream:
a hand on our numb fingers,
a light in the cabin window,
remembered voices.

VIRGINIA HAMILTON ADAIR was born in 1913 in New York City. Educated at Kimberly, Mount Holyoke, Radcliffe, and the University of Wisconsin, she taught briefly at Wisconsin, the College of William & Mary, and Pomona College, and for twenty-two years at California Polytechnic University at Pomona. She lives in Claremont, California.

This book was set in Granjon, a modern recutting of a typeface produced under the direction of George W. Jones, who based Granjon's design upon the letter forms of Claude Garamond (1480–1561). The name was given to the typeface as a tribute to the typographic designer Robert Granjon.

Made in the USA
San Bernardino, CA
11 April 2015